Dear Sophie,
Love from Mum x

Eva & Maxime dis

THE D-DAY LANDINGS

Story written by
A. Derreumaux & L. Granier
& drawn by J. Mauduit

OREP
EDITIONS

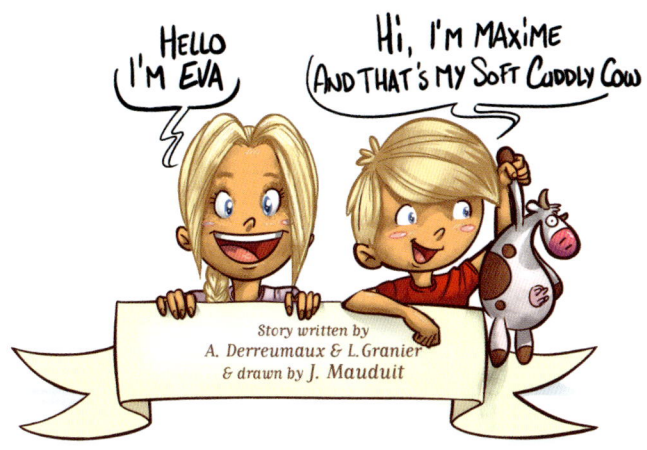

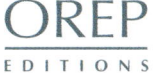

Eva and Maxime live in a large house by the sea in Normandy.

They absolutely love it and find it really pretty!

It's a house with wooden beams, lovely flowers growing on the roof, and a fireplace to light a fire when it's cold...

Did you know?

From 1939 to 1945, the world was at war: it was World War II. Several countries were involved, including France which was partly occupied by the German army. From June 1944, Normandy played a highly important role in the outcome of this war.

Did you know?

*During the war, there were two sides: the Allies and the Axis.
The Allies included the United States, the Soviet Union
and the United Kingdom.
The Axis was comprised of Germany, Italy and Japan.*

One day, they saw their small town totally transformed!

People had attached large flags to their house windows, in the sky, planes were flying by at lightning speed, and the sea was filled with huge warships.

Eva and Maxime could hardly believe their eyes...

What was happening on the Normandy beaches?

We're going to celebrate the D-Day Landings,' grandma replied.

'*The D-Day Landings?*' Eva asked. '*What's that?*'

'*Let me explain.*'

They came across a fine seafront villa.

*'This is where I lived as a child,' Grandma told them.
'I was the same age as you, Eva...'*

'Why did you change houses? This one is very nice!'

*It was a long, long time ago, sweetheart, back in 1940.
We lived here happily with my parents and my brothers.
We played hopscotch and with hoops, or hide and seek
in the garden... a bit like you do today!'*

Did you know?

The flags are those of the leading countries that took part in the Landings: the United States, the United Kingdom and Canada. Franklin Roosevelt was the President of the United States, and Winston Churchill, the British Prime Minister, was also in charge of the Canadian army.

Franklin Roosevelt
President of the United-States
from 1933 to 1945

'But, one day, men in uniforms arrived: they were German officers. They told us that, from now on, we must obey them.'

'Why?' Maxime worriedly enquired.

'Their chief, Hitler, wanted his country to become greater and richer. So, he decided to invade France, but also Europe.

Our lives changed a great deal...Such was the war...'

Did you know?

Adolf Hitler was the German chancellor. He was the leader of Nazi Germany and he created the Nazi party. The swastika was this party's symbol.

Adolf Hitler
Chancellor of Germany

'What's the war, grandma?' Maxime asked.

'The war is when people who don't agree fight with each other. They use weapons, people die and many families are forced to leave their homes. The war is terrible...'

Did you know?

Several houses were destroyed by the bombardments, whereas others were occupied by the German army. Families were therefore obliged to leave their homes and to take to the road or to seek refuge, in nearby farms or quarries (i.e. grottos) for example - this is what we call 'the exodus'.

'In France,' grandma continued, 'some people wanted to prevent the German army from advancing. They created a group called the Resistance.'

'And what did they do?' Eva asked.

'They helped people who were hungry to find food, they blew up the trains that were transporting weapons for the German army...'

'Were all the Germans nasty?'

'No, of course not, darling... There were also Germans who did not like Hitler.'

Did you know?

On the 22nd of June 1940, the French Marshal Pétain signed the armistice: the war was over, but France was still occupied by the German army. France was divided in two: the occupied zone in the north and the free zone in the south. General de Gaulle organised the Resistance from London, in England.

Charles De Gaulle
French army general

'*Then what happened?*' asked Maxime.

'*British, American and Canadian soldiers, but also those from other nations, came to fight to liberate France and Europe. They arrived on our beaches, in Normandy, with boats, planes and weapons. That's what we now call the D-Day Landings. And they happened on the 6th of June 1944. I'll never forget that date.*'

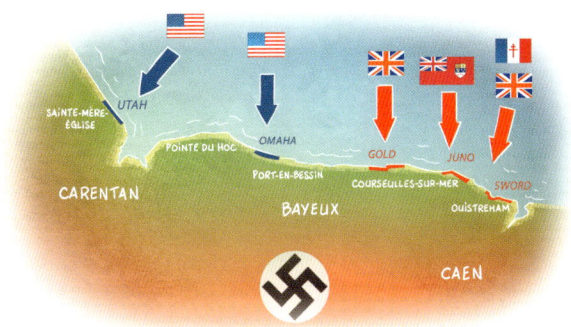

Did you know?

The Allies landed on five beaches: Utah and Omaha Beach for the Americans, Gold and Sword for the British, and Juno Beach for the Canadians. Hence, the Battle of Normandy had begun.

Dwight D. Eisenhower
American army general

'*So, the war was over then?*' asked Maxime.

'*Oh no, not at all honey... On the night of the 5th to the 6th of June, Allied soldiers captured the bridge we now call Pegasus Bridge. Then they liberated the towns of Bayeux and Caen, then Paris and the rest of Europe.*'

Did you know?

The name '*Pegasus Bridge*' *was given in honour of the British parachutists whose emblem was Pegasus, the winged horse.*

'In Arromanches,' grandma continued, *'the Allies then built an artificial harbour, the remains of which we can still see today.'*

'What did they use the harbour for?' Eva then asked.

'To keep fighting, the soldiers needed new weapons and food. It was all shipped over from England. The boats that transported all this material arrived in Arromanches, where the harbour had been specially built. The material was then issued to the soldiers.'

Did you know?

The artificial harbour in Arromanches was given the codename Mulberry. *This is why it is still sometimes referred to as* 'Port Mulberry'.

'But, since it was the war,' Eva continued, rather surprised, *'why are we celebrating today?'*

'After the D-Day Landings, France and Europe were liberated and we regained our freedom. Times were still complicated, for many houses had been destroyed and it was not always easy to find food in grocery stores... but we were free again. And it's that newfound freedom that we are celebrating today. It's very important that we never forget that period of our history, so that war may never ever happen again. Peace is such a fragile thing...'

Did you know?

To ensure the Landings were a success, three conditions were necessary: 1/ the Germans needed to be taken by surprise, 2/ the tide needed to be rising and 3/ the storm needed to calm down. All of these conditions were reunited on the 6th of June.

Winston Churchill
Prime Minister of the United Kingdom

Eva and Maxime admired the huge procession of soldiers who had come from the world over. They were carrying large flags and wearing fine uniforms.

'*These soldiers*, grandma explained, '*are from all the countries that were involved in World War II. They are marching together as a sign of the reconciliation of all the states that were once at war. It's their way of showing that we can build a better world together. And the very serious people in the stands are the presidents of all those countries.*'

When the procession was over, children of different nationalities held hands and formed a circle on the beach. Grandma was quite emotional as she watched Eva and Maxime join them. Despite the small tears that ran down her cheeks, her face lit up with a huge smile.

'*Children,* she whispered, '*never forget... that whether you come from France, Germany, the United States or elsewhere, you are always bearers of peace. It's thanks to you that we can continue to live free and united.*'

Did you know?

After World War II, a flag was created to symbolise the united countries of Europe: a circle with 12 gold stars on a blue background. The stars symbolise unity, solidarity and harmony. The flag was adopted in 1955. Europe's hymn is The Ode to Joy *by Beethoven.*

THE ARTIFICIAL HARBOUR IN ARROMANCHES

EVA AND MAXIME'S ADVICE

In Normandy, there are several sites that remind us of World War II and that contribute towards remembrance. Here are a few:

- *the D-Day landing beaches: Omaha Beach, Utah Beach, Gold Beach, Sword Beach and Juno Beach;*
- *the artificial harbour in Arromanches;*
- *Pegasus Bridge in Bénouville;*
- *war cemeteries;*
- *bunkers along the Atlantic Wall;*
- *Sainte-Mère-Église.*